Copyright: Really Useful Map Company (HK) Ltd.
Published by Robert Frederick Ltd.
4 North Parade Bath, England.
First Published: 2005

Designed and packaged by
**Q2A Creative**
Printed in China

# DISCOVER SHARKS

# Contents

# A Shark's Tale

Sharks are amongst the most feared creatures on Earth, and only the very brave dare to go near them. They are meat lovers and have been around since before even the dinosaurs! Found in oceans, seas and rivers, they rule the waters with their sharp teeth and swift movements. Sharks are related to fish, yet they differ in many ways.

## Bony matters

While most fish have skeletons made of bones, the shark skeleton is made up entirely of cartilage. Cartilage is the same flexible material that is found inside your ears and nose. It makes the shark lighter in weight and helps it to swim faster.

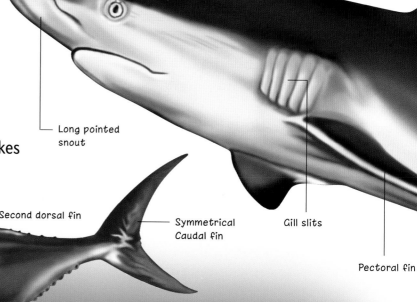

Dorsal fin

Long pointed snout

Gill slits

Pectoral fin

First dorsal fin

Second dorsal fin

Symmetrical Caudal fin

Barbel

Pectoral fin

Most fish have bony skeletons

## Living dens

Shark can be found in most oceans and seas. Large and more active sharks usually stay near the surface or the middle of the ocean. The smaller ones prefer the ocean floor. Some sharks live near the coast and can ev enter rivers and lakes that a linked to the sea.

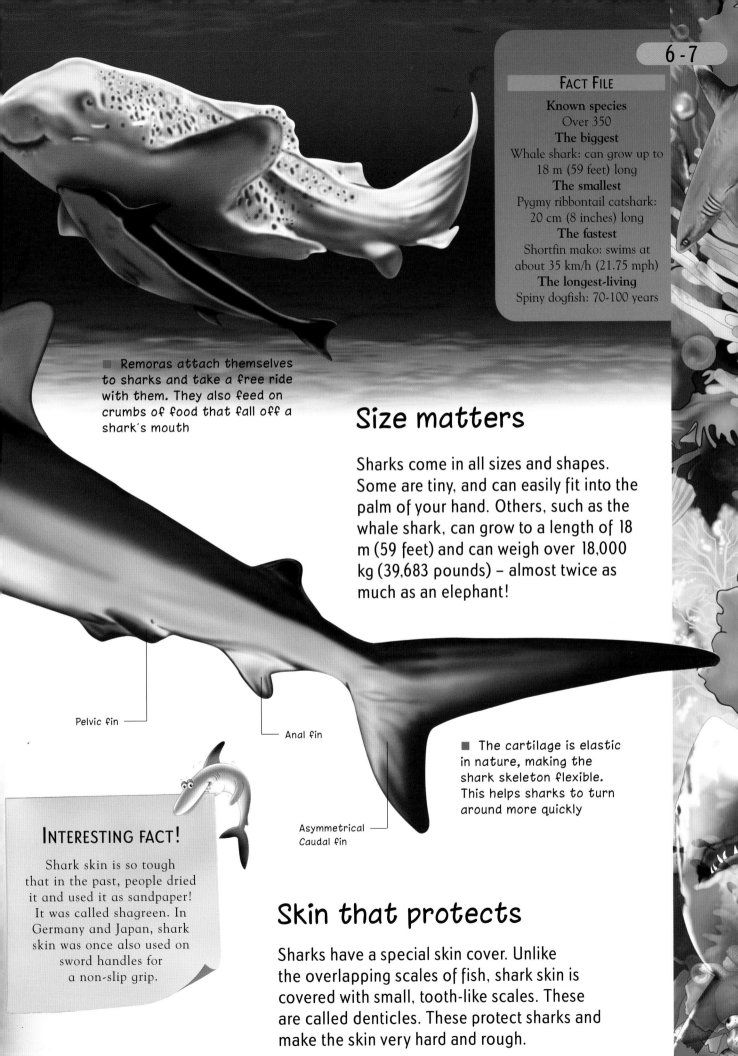

## FACT FILE

**Known species**
Over 350
**The biggest**
Whale shark: can grow up to
18 m (59 feet) long
**The smallest**
Pygmy ribbontail catshark:
20 cm (8 inches) long
**The fastest**
Shortfin mako: swims at
about 35 km/h (21.75 mph)
**The longest-living**
Spiny dogfish: 70-100 years

■ Remoras attach themselves
to sharks and take a free ride
with them. They also feed on
crumbs of food that fall off a
shark's mouth

# Size matters

Sharks come in all sizes and shapes.
Some are tiny, and can easily fit into the
palm of your hand. Others, such as the
whale shark, can grow to a length of 18
m (59 feet) and can weigh over 18,000
kg (39,683 pounds) – almost twice as
much as an elephant!

Pelvic fin

Anal fin

■ The cartilage is elastic
in nature, making the
shark skeleton flexible.
This helps sharks to turn
around more quickly

Asymmetrical
Caudal fin

## INTERESTING FACT!

Shark skin is so tough
that in the past, people dried
it and used it as sandpaper!
It was called shagreen. In
Germany and Japan, shark
skin was once also used on
sword handles for
a non-slip grip.

# Skin that protects

Sharks have a special skin cover. Unlike
the overlapping scales of fish, shark skin is
covered with small, tooth-like scales. These
are called denticles. These protect sharks and
make the skin very hard and rough.

# In the Beginning...

Most creatures go through evolution, or change their features to adapt to their environment. But sharks are good survivors and have had little need to change in the last 150 million years.

## Few fossils

Fossils are the dead remains of animals that stay preserved for hundreds of millions of years. Fossils have helped us study evolution. But a shark's skeleton crumbles quickly, as it is made of cartilage. Complete shark fossils, therefore, have not been found. All the fossils that have been found have been limited to their teeth and spines from their fins.

■ The Helicoprions lived 250 million years ago. Their jaws had a spiral-tooth setting, with smaller teeth on the front and larger ones at the back

## Earliest sharks

Scientists believe that the ancestors of modern-day sharks appeared 350 to 400 million years ago, a time known as the Age of Fish, or the Devonian Period. This was 100 million years before dinosaurs existed. The earliest shark fossils are found in Antarctica and Australia.

INTERESTING FACT!

It is believed that extinct sharks had short, round snouts, while most modern sharks have slightly long and pointed snouts. Some even have saw-like snouts.

■ The Orthacanthus lived in fresh waters and had V-shaped teeth. This species is now extinct

**FACT FILE**

**MEGALODON**
**Tooth size**
Around 15 cm
(6 inches) long
**Was found around**
Europe, India,
Australia, America
**Weighed**
Over 35 tons (77,162
pounds), equal to the weight
of 12 elephants
**Length**
More than 16 m (52.5 feet)
**Jaws opened up**
1.8 m (6 feet) wide and
2.1 m (7 feet) high

■ A tooth belonging
to the Megalodon

■ A full-grown
human, standing
at 1.8 m (6 feet),
would have been
just as big as the
Megalodon's fin

## The mega monster

One extinct shark known for its huge fossil teeth is the Megalodon.
It lived between 25 to 1.6 million years ago. Each of the Megalodon's
teeth was the size of a full-grown person's hand! Scientists believe it
was probably longer than 16 m (52.5 feet). It may have been similar
to the great white shark and was known to feed on whales.

## Modern sharks

Most modern-day sharks stopped evolving a long time ago. They have changed
very little in the last 100 million years. But scientists are still not sure about how
many kinds of sharks exist today. They continue to discover new species.

# Body Basics

Living in the water can be tough. To meet this challenge, sharks are equipped with special features. All sharks have strong jaws, a pair of fins and nostrils and a flexible skeleton. Sharks are great swimmers but, unlike fish, they cannot move backwards.

## Colouring effect

Shark skin is double shaded, with the top side being darker than the belly. When the shark is seen from above, its upper surface appears to resemble the dark ocean floor. Seen from below, the belly blends in with the light above. This helps the shark to hunt without being noticed.

### INTERESTING FACT!

A shark's tongue is very different from a human one. Found on the floor of the mouth, it is small, thick and mostly still. It is called a basihyal. Some sharks use it to rip the flesh off their prey.

■ The anatomy of sharks varies according to their habitats. Sharks living in deeper oceans have larger eyes than those found near the ocean surface

■ Unlike the gills of bony fish, shark gills do not have covers. Water must continue to flow across the gill slits for the shark to breathe

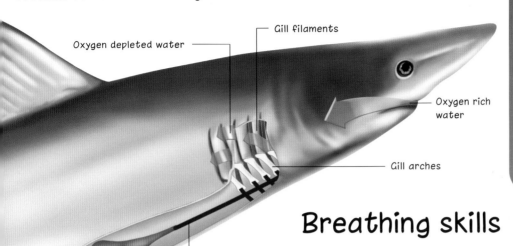

Gill filaments

Oxygen depleted water

Oxygen rich water

Gill arches

Heart

Ventral aorta

# Breathing skills

Sharks, like fish, take oxygen from water. They have gill slits on either side of their heads. Water enters these slits and passes over the gill chambers, where oxygen is absorbed. Some sharks need to swim continuously to breathe, while others open and close their mouths to pump the water in.

■ Most sharks have five pairs of gills, while bony fish have just one. The broadnose sevengill shark, however, has seven pairs of gills

# Oil Tank!

The largest organ in a shark is the liver, which is filled with oil. Since oil is lighter than water, it keeps the shark from sinking. Despite this, sharks must swim constantly to keep afloat. The liver also functions as a storehouse of energy.

# Torpedo-like!

Most sharks have a rounded body that tapers at both ends. This torpedo-like shape helps them while swimming. But some sharks, like the angelshark, have a flat body. This helps them to live at the bottom of the ocean.

■ Sharks usually have blunt snouts. But sawsharks have long snouts with toothed edges, which help them to dig out prey from the ocean floor or to slash at fish passing by

■ The unique shape of the hammerhead shark's head helps it to get a better view of its surroundings

# Shark Senses

Sharks have all the senses that humans do – and something extra too! Sharks can not only smell, see, feel, hear and taste. They also have a sixth sense. Their senses help them to hunt and travel great distances.

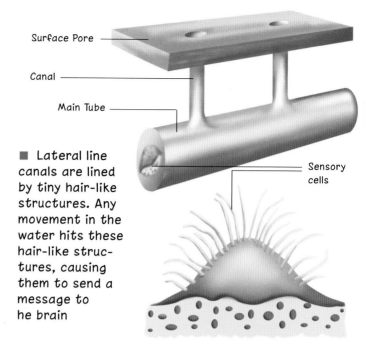

■ Lateral line canals are lined by tiny hair-like structures. Any movement in the water hits these hair-like structures, causing them to send a message to he brain

Surface Pore

Canal

Main Tube

Sensory cells

## Line of action

Sharks have fluid-filled canals that run from head to toe on both sides of their body. This is called the lateral line. It enables the shark to sense movements in water. Some scientists believe that the lateral line can also detect low sounds.

## Sixth sense

While electricity usually comes from wires and batteries, all living creatures also produce weak electric fields. Sharks are able to detect these with the help of their sixth sense. Tiny pores on the shark's snout lead to jelly-filled sacs known as the ampullae of Lorenzini that help them detect electrical fields.

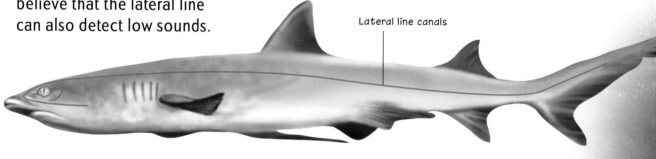

Lateral line canals

## Smelly matters

In general, the nostrils of sharks are located on the underside of their snouts. They are used for smelling and not for breathing. Some sharks have nasal barbels, which look like thick whiskers sticking out from the bottom of the snout. Barbels help the shark to feel and taste.

■ Blind sharks cannot see. They hunt for their prey by using their nasal barbels

■ Certain sharks, such as the nurse
shark, have openings called spiracles
just behind their eyes. The shark
uses these spiracles to breathe
while hunting or feeding

# Looking on

Sharks have very good eyesight, even better than
ours. A shark's eye, like that of a cat, can contract
or expand according to the light. This helps them
to see in dim light. Sharks can also see colours.

## INTERESTING FACT!

Sharks do not have
external ear flaps. Instead,
their ears are inside their
heads, on both sides of the
brain case. Each ear leads
to a small pore on the
shark's head.

■ The great white shark has
a keen sense of smell. It can
detect a drop of blood in
100 litres (176 pints) of water!

# Toothy Terrors

A shark's only proper weapon is its mouth. The mouth is below the snout in all species except the angelshark, the megamouth, whale shark and wobbegong shark. These species have their mouths at the end of their snouts. The two most important parts of a shark's mouth are the teeth and the jaws.

## Tearing and crushing

Sharks do not chew their food, but gulp it down whole. They use their teeth only to tear the food into mouth-sized pieces. Some sharks also crush the shell of their prey with their teeth.

## Big bite

In most animals, the lower jaw moves freely, but the upper jaw is attached to the skull. However, in sharks, the upper jaw rests below the skull. It moves out when the shark attacks its prey. This allows the shark to push its entire mouth forward to grab its victim. As the lower jaw teeth puncture and hold the prey, the upper jaw teeth slice it.

■ The great white has large wedge-shaped teeth with jagged edges. The teeth of the Megalodon were three times larger than those of the great white

Great White Shark

Sand tiger

Mako

■ Different types of shark teeth

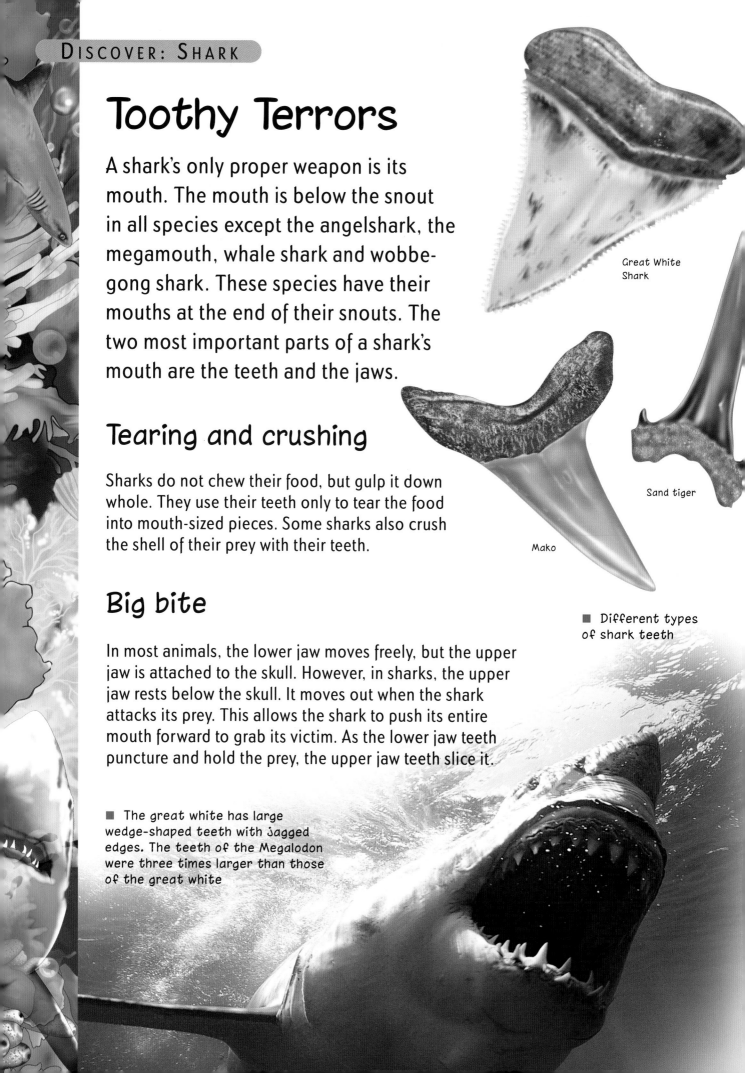

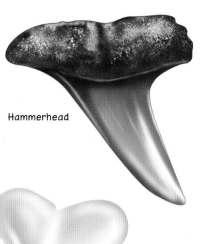
Hammerhead

Blue Shark

FACT FILE

**Number of teeth**
Over 3,000
**For a bite**
5-15 rows of teeth
**Teeth replaced every**
10-21 days
**Largest tooth is the
Megalodon's, at nearly**
15 cm (6 inches)
**Bite strength**
Average of 25,000 pounds
per sq in

# Sharp new ones

Shark teeth fall out all the time. This is crucial, as worn out or broken teeth are continually replaced by new and sharper ones. The process takes place as often as every two weeks. In some sharks, like the great white, these teeth are arranged in several rows.

# Tooth types

Sharks have a variety of teeth. Some have molar-like teeth, which help in the process of grinding. Others have razor-like cutting or pointed teeth.

■ Cookie-cutter sharks eat their prey by attaching themselves to it with special sucking lips. Once attached, they roll their body to cut out a chunk of flesh!

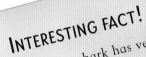

## INTERESTING FACT!

The basking shark has very tiny teeth. It does not use them to feed. Instead, the shark swallows plankton-rich water. Special bristles inside its mouth, called gill rakers, filter this food as the water flows through them.

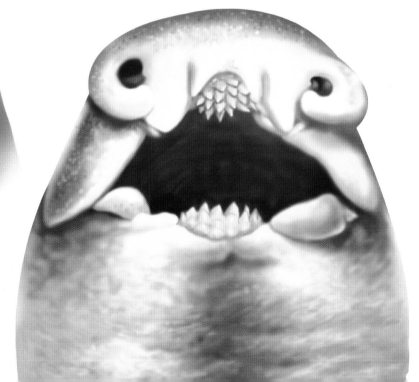

■ The Port Jackson shark does not have jagged teeth. Its front teeth are pointed for grasping its prey, while the back teeth are flat and molar-like for crushing

# Young Ones

Baby sharks are called pups. A single litter could contain more than 100 pups! There are three different ways in which shark pups are born.

## Laying eggs

Some sharks lay eggs like birds. The mother deposits the egg cases in the sea. The baby inside the egg gets its food from the yolk until the egg hatches. The parents do not protect the eggs. Horn sharks and swell sharks are egg-laying sharks. Such sharks are known as oviparous sharks.

## Birth of a shark

Sharks like the hammerhead give birth to pups. The eggs hatch inside the mother's body and the babies get their food from the mother directly. Sharks that give birth to their young in this manner are called viviparous sharks. Lemon sharks, hammerheads, bull sharks and whale sharks are all types of viviparous sharks.

■ Horn shark eggs are spiral shaped and hatch six to nine months after being laid. The pups are usually 15-17 cm (5.9-6.7 inches) long

■ Certain shark's eggs are also called mermaid's purses because of their pouch-like appearance. The egg contains yolk that the baby feeds on

# Hatching inside

In some sharks, although the eggs hatch inside the mother, the young ones do not get nourishment directly from their mother. Instead, the babies feed off other unfertilised eggs. At times, they even eat up their brothers and sisters! This kind of reproduction is called ovoviviparity.

■ A shark giving birth. The newborn pup lies on the ocean floor for a while after it's born. It then pulls against the cord that links it to its mother. Once the cord breaks, the young one swims away

## INTERESTING FACT!

Shark eggs are enclosed in a tough leathery membrane. They can be of various shapes – pouch-like or shaped like a screw. Some even have tendrils that attach themselves to seaweeds and rocks on the ocean floor.

# Caring for babies

Sharks do not care for their babies. The young sharks are well-equipped to look after themselves. In fact, they swim away from their mothers as soon as they are born. Sometimes a mother can even eat her newborn pups.

■ The predators of young sharks include larger sharks and killer whales. Some small sharks are even eaten by huge fish like the giant grouper

# Giants of the Deep

Huge sharks have dominated the oceans of the world for centuries. The largest-ever shark is probably the now-extinct Megalodon. Some believe that the shark was over 18 m (60 feet) in length, and weighed as much as 12 elephants! Amongst the modern sharks, the largest are the whale and basking sharks.

## Not a whale!

Contrary to what its name suggests, the whale shark is not a whale. It is a shark that is, at times, as big as a school bus! The whale shark has a huge mouth that may measure up to 1m (4 feet).

## Straining food

Whale and basking sharks feed on plankton by straining the tiny marine plants and animals from the water. They swim with their mouth open and suck in water filled with plankton. The shark then filters its food through special bristles attached to the gills and swallows the food. The water is thrown out through the gill slits.

### INTERESTING FACT!

Both whale and basking sharks are slow swimmers. They swim by moving their body from side to side. Neither of these sharks harms humans.

Whale shark

# Colourful skins

Whale sharks have light-grey skin with yellow dots and stripes. On the other hand, basking sharks are darker in colour. They are greyish-brown to black or bluish on the upper surface, while their belly is off-white in colour.

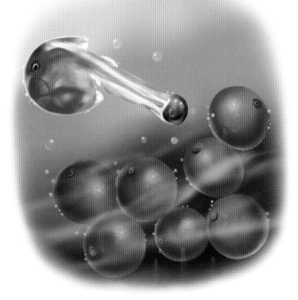

■ Whale sharks love fish eggs. They are known to wait for hours for fish to lay eggs so that they can eat them. They even return year after year to the same mating grounds where the fish release their eggs into the water

# The big basking

The basking shark is the second-largest shark. It has a short and conical snout. Unlike whale sharks that travel alone, basking sharks often move around in schools of 100 members.

■ Basking sharks are so called because they cruise slowly along the ocean surface. This gives them the appearance of basking in the sun

# Pygmies of the Deep

Not all sharks are huge monsters. Some are, in fact, so small that they can fit into your hand! The smallest sharks include the pygmy ribbontail catshark, dwarf lanternshark and the spined pygmy shark. But like their bigger siblings, small sharks have strong teeth, and a bite from them can be decidedly painful!

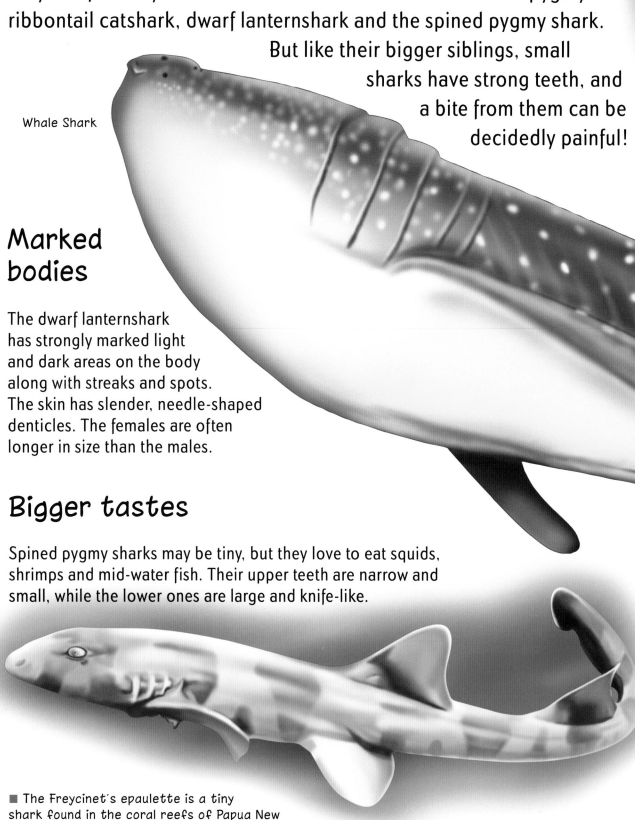

Whale Shark

## Marked bodies

The dwarf lanternshark has strongly marked light and dark areas on the body along with streaks and spots. The skin has slender, needle-shaped denticles. The females are often longer in size than the males.

## Bigger tastes

Spined pygmy sharks may be tiny, but they love to eat squids, shrimps and mid-water fish. Their upper teeth are narrow and small, while the lower ones are large and knife-like.

■ The Freycinet's epaulette is a tiny shark found in the coral reefs of Papua New Guinea. It hides during the day and hunts at night

# Tiny and glowing

Spined pygmy sharks are very sleek and have a bulb-like snout. They are dark grey to black in colour and have white-tipped fins. Their bellies actually glow in the dark. They live in deep waters and are rarely seen.

■ The pygmy ribbontail catshark lives on the muddy ocean floor, on slopes and outer shelves. It looks tiny compared to the huge whale shark

## INTERESTING FACT!

Spined pygmy sharks are commonly found at the bottom of the ocean. However, these sharks are known to journey up to about 198 m (650 feet) at night to hunt in the mid-water zones.

# Ribbons undersea

Pygmy ribbontail catsharks are dark brown in colour with blackish markings on the fins. They are found around Tanzania, India, Vietnam and the Philippines. The small shark feeds on small bony fish and crustaceans.

# The Great White Shark

Infamous for its appearance in the movie *Jaws* as a bloodthirsty man-eater, the great white shark is the largest predatory shark. The name *Jaws* was apt, given that this shark has as many as 3,000 razor-sharp teeth! It grows to over 4.5 m (14.7 feet) in length and weighs as much as 1,360 kg (3,000 pounds)! The great white is also known as the "white pointer" and "white death".

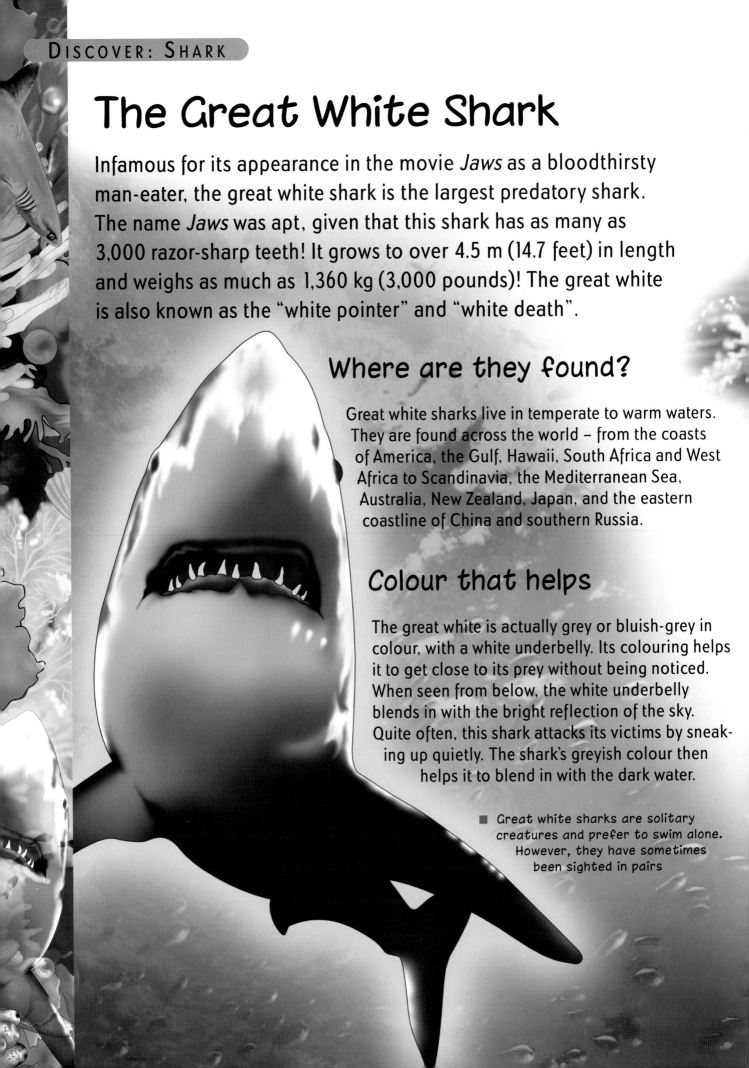

## Where are they found?

Great white sharks live in temperate to warm waters. They are found across the world – from the coasts of America, the Gulf, Hawaii, South Africa and West Africa to Scandinavia, the Mediterranean Sea, Australia, New Zealand, Japan, and the eastern coastline of China and southern Russia.

## Colour that helps

The great white is actually grey or bluish-grey in colour, with a white underbelly. Its colouring helps it to get close to its prey without being noticed. When seen from below, the white underbelly blends in with the bright reflection of the sky. Quite often, this shark attacks its victims by sneaking up quietly. The shark's greyish colour then helps it to blend in with the dark water.

■ Great white sharks are solitary creatures and prefer to swim alone. However, they have sometimes been sighted in pairs

# Fierce bite

With a mouth that is most often open, you cannot miss the rows of white, triangle-shaped, razor-sharp teeth. The shark's teeth can grow up to 7.5 cm (3 inches) long. Old or broken teeth are replaced by a row of new teeth.

## HABITAT

## FACT FILE

**Average length**
3.6-4.9 m (12-16 feet)
**Can grow up to**
6.8 m (22.3 feet)
**Can be as heavy as**
3,312 kg (7,302 pounds)
**Number of babies**
2-14 pups
**Shark attack**
30-50 attacks per year
**Fatal attacks**
10-15 deaths every year
**Can swim as deep as**
250 m (775 feet)

## INTERESTING FACT!

Great white sharks are ovoviviparous. The eggs of the great white remain inside the body of the female shark until they hatch. The female then gives birth to live young ones.

■ Great white sharks often jump out of the water while chasing seals. This is breaching

# What do they eat?

Great whites eat dolphins, sea lions, seals, big bony fish and even penguins. Though they have earned a reputation for being man-eaters, they do not usually attack humans. These sharks are also scavengers, as they eat dead animals that float in water.

The great white first attacks its victim, injures it and then moves away. He approaches it later, when the pain and bleeding has weakened it. The shark does not chew its food, but rips the prey into mouth-sized pieces before swallowing them. After a good meal, this shark can do without another one for over a month!

■ Great whites are known to attack pelicans, but they prefer to eat seals

# Tiger Sharks and Bull Sharks

Many sharks, like the tiger and bull sharks, are named after land animals. The tiger shark has dark stripes on its back, similar to the big cat. But as the shark grows older, the stripes often fade away. The bull shark gets its name from its flat, wide and short snout, which resembles that of a bull.

■ Tiger sharks have good eyesight, which is aided by a special gill slit called a spiracle. Located behind the eye, this slit provides oxygen directly to the eyes and the brain

## Tough tigers

The tiger shark has a very large mouth with powerful jaws. The triangular teeth of these sharks have saw-like edges that can slice through many objects. The tiger shark is not a very fast swimmer and often hunts at night.

## Junk eaters

Tiger sharks love food and will eat almost anything. Biologists have found alarm clocks, tin cans, deer antlers and even shoes in the stomach of dead tiger sharks! Tiger sharks also feed on other sharks, fish, turtles and crabs.

■ Tiger sharks often prey on albatross chicks, which fall into the ocean while learning to fly

# Bull sharks

The bull shark lives near coastal areas. It is also commonly found in rivers and freshwater lakes. Bull sharks eat fish, other sharks, turtles, birds and dolphins. Interestingly, adult female bull sharks are longer in size than male bull sharks.

## FACT FILE

Tiger sharks are as long as 6 m (20 feet)
Bull sharks measure up to 3.5 m (11.5 feet)
Tiger sharks can live up to 30-40 years
Bull sharks can live up to 14 years
Tiger sharks swim at 3.9 km/h (2.4 mph)

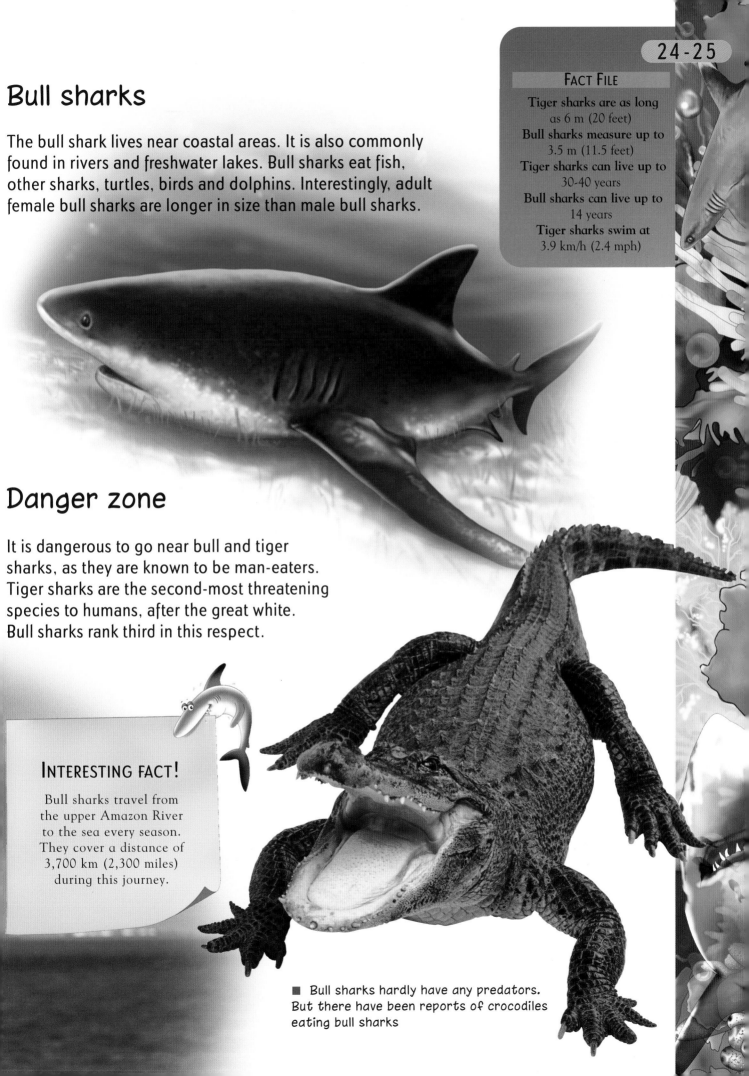

# Danger zone

It is dangerous to go near bull and tiger sharks, as they are known to be man-eaters. Tiger sharks are the second-most threatening species to humans, after the great white. Bull sharks rank third in this respect.

## INTERESTING FACT!

Bull sharks travel from the upper Amazon River to the sea every season. They cover a distance of 3,700 km (2,300 miles) during this journey.

■ Bull sharks hardly have any predators. But there have been reports of crocodiles eating bull sharks

# The Swift Mako

Sharks are great swimmers, and the fastest among them is the mako. Makos can swim at speeds ranging from 35.4 km/h (22 mph) and 96.5 km/h (60 mph). These sharks also leap out of the waters, jumping to a height of 1.83 m (6 feet). They are even known to jump into boats!

## Shaped for speed

Makos are fast swimmers because of their sleek, spindle-like shape. They also have a long and conical snout. Their side fins are short and the tail fin is crescent-shaped to provide more power while swimming.

## Other relatives

Makos belong to the order of mackerel sharks. Other sharks in this order include the great white, the porbeagle and the sand tiger shark. Sand tiger sharks are also called grey nurse sharks. They are found in most warm seas around the world. The porbeagle gets its name from its porpoise-like shape.

■ The sand tiger shark is known to swim to the surface and take huge gulps of air. It holds the air in its stomach to lie motionless in the water

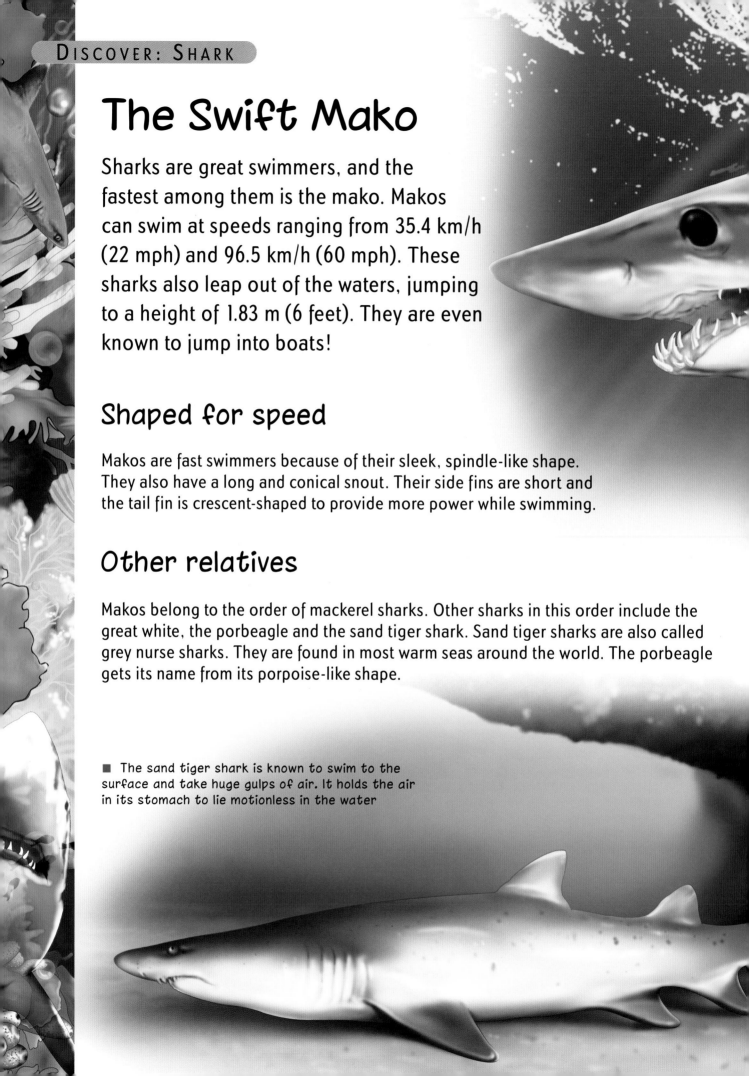

## HABITAT

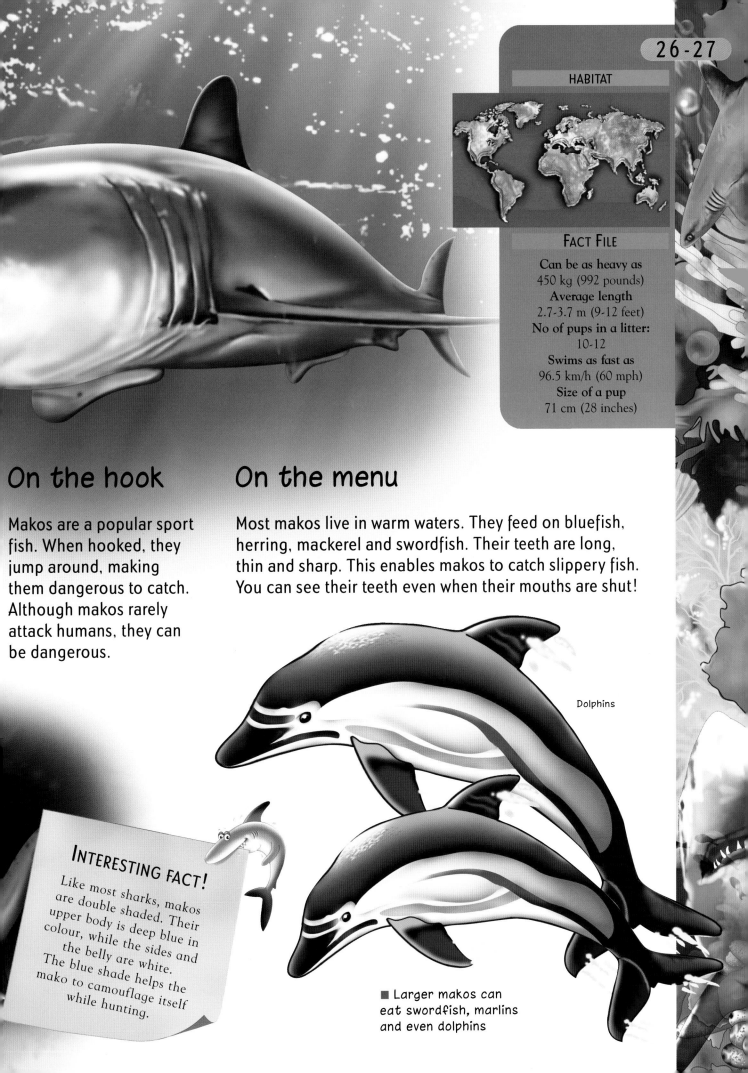

### FACT FILE

Can be as heavy as
450 kg (992 pounds)
Average length
2.7-3.7 m (9-12 feet)
No of pups in a litter:
10-12
Swims as fast as
96.5 km/h (60 mph)
Size of a pup
71 cm (28 inches)

# On the hook

Makos are a popular sport fish. When hooked, they jump around, making them dangerous to catch. Although makos rarely attack humans, they can be dangerous.

# On the menu

Most makos live in warm waters. They feed on bluefish, herring, mackerel and swordfish. Their teeth are long, thin and sharp. This enables makos to catch slippery fish. You can see their teeth even when their mouths are shut!

Dolphins

### INTERESTING FACT!

Like most sharks, makos are double shaded. Their upper body is deep blue in colour, while the sides and the belly are white. The blue shade helps the mako to camouflage itself while hunting.

■ Larger makos can eat swordfish, marlins and even dolphins

# Ground Sharks

Ground sharks are the most common type of sharks. They have long snouts and a mouth that reaches behind the eyes. Their eyes are special too. Ground shark eyes have a lower eyelid that moves to cover the eyes during hunting. Ground sharks include hammerhead, carpet and swell sharks and all the requiem sharks, such as the tiger, blue, lemon, bull and certain reef sharks.

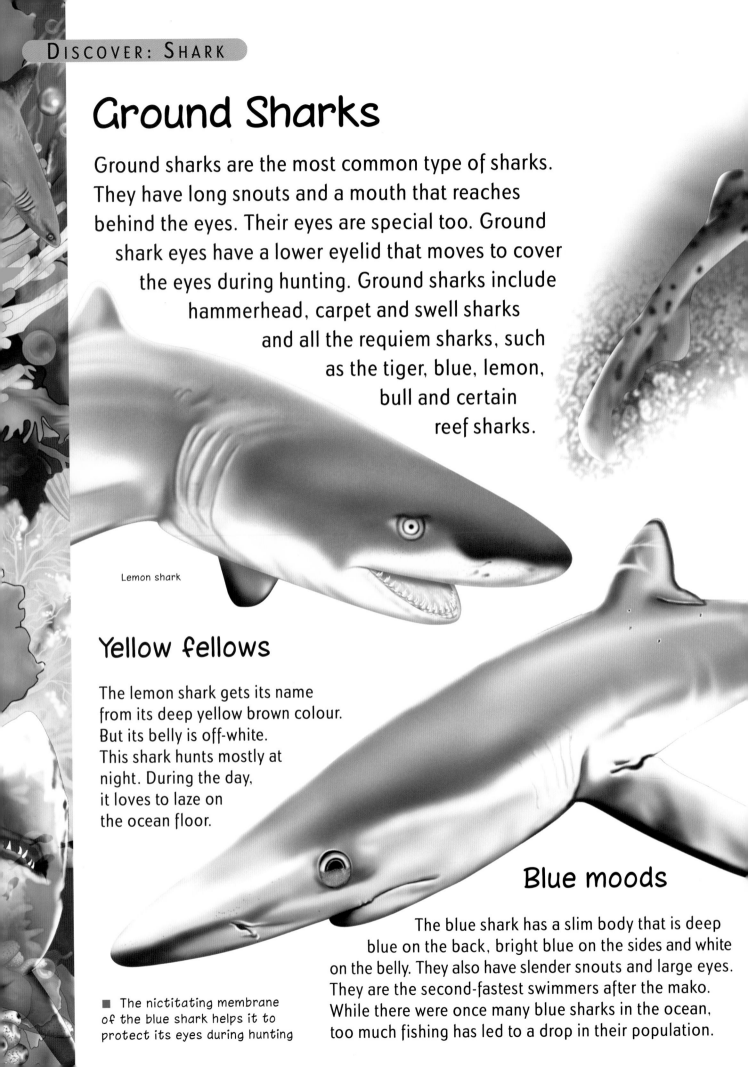

Lemon shark

## Yellow fellows

The lemon shark gets its name from its deep yellow brown colour. But its belly is off-white. This shark hunts mostly at night. During the day, it loves to laze on the ocean floor.

## Blue moods

The blue shark has a slim body that is deep blue on the back, bright blue on the sides and white on the belly. They also have slender snouts and large eyes. They are the second-fastest swimmers after the mako. While there were once many blue sharks in the ocean, too much fishing has led to a drop in their population.

■ The nictitating membrane of the blue shark helps it to protect its eyes during hunting

■ The swell shark can increase the size of its body by swallowing large amounts of water. This scares away the shark's enemies

# Danger factor

Lemon sharks live near the surface and are often seen at bays, docks and river mouths. Though they swim close to human areas, lemon sharks attack only if provoked. Meanwhile, blue sharks live far away from the shores, and yet are known to attack humans.

## INTERESTING FACT!

The blue shark migrates the longest distances. It travels 2,000-3,000 km (1,200-1,700 miles) in a seasonal journey from New York State in the US to Brazil.

■ While most sharks eat other sea animals, Californian sea lions love to feed on young blue sharks

# No fuss about food

Blue sharks can eat anything, but they prefer squids and fish. On the other hand, the lemon shark likes to feed on crabs, rays, shrimps, sea birds and smaller sharks.

# Reef Sharks

Sharks live in different zones and regions of the ocean. Some, such as blacktip, whitetip and Caribbean reef sharks, live near coral reefs. Divers and waders often come into contact with such sharks.

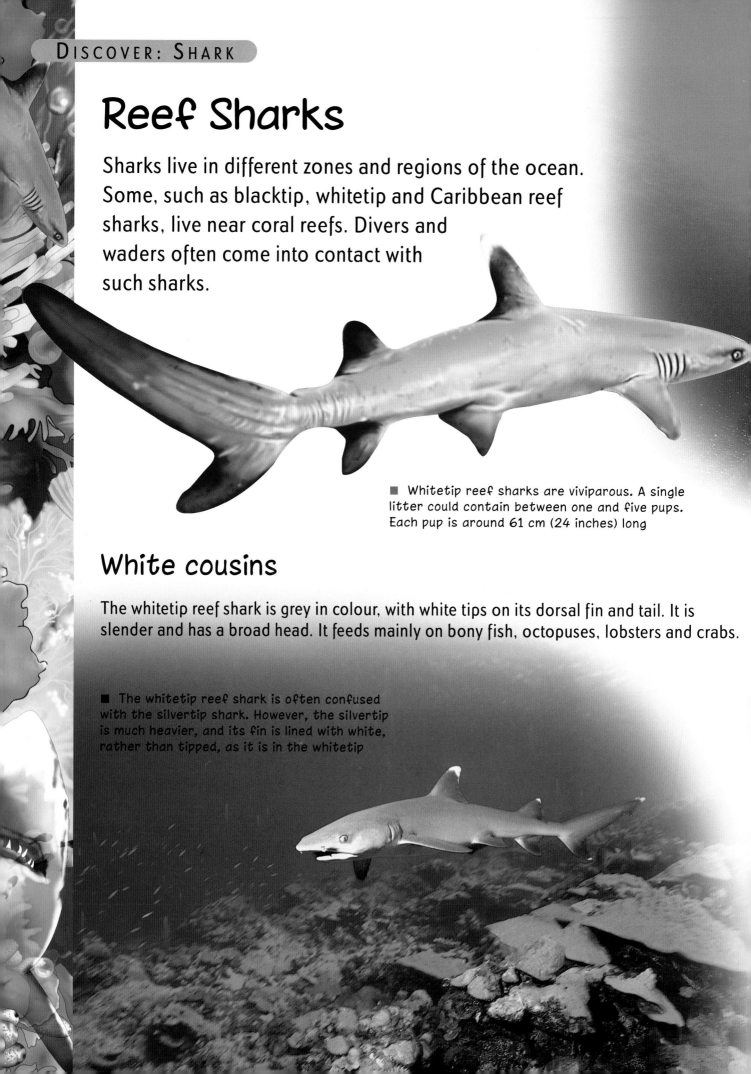

■ Whitetip reef sharks are viviparous. A single litter could contain between one and five pups. Each pup is around 61 cm (24 inches) long

## White cousins

The whitetip reef shark is grey in colour, with white tips on its dorsal fin and tail. It is slender and has a broad head. It feeds mainly on bony fish, octopuses, lobsters and crabs.

■ The whitetip reef shark is often confused with the silvertip shark. However, the silvertip is much heavier, and its fin is lined with white, rather than tipped, as it is in the whitetip

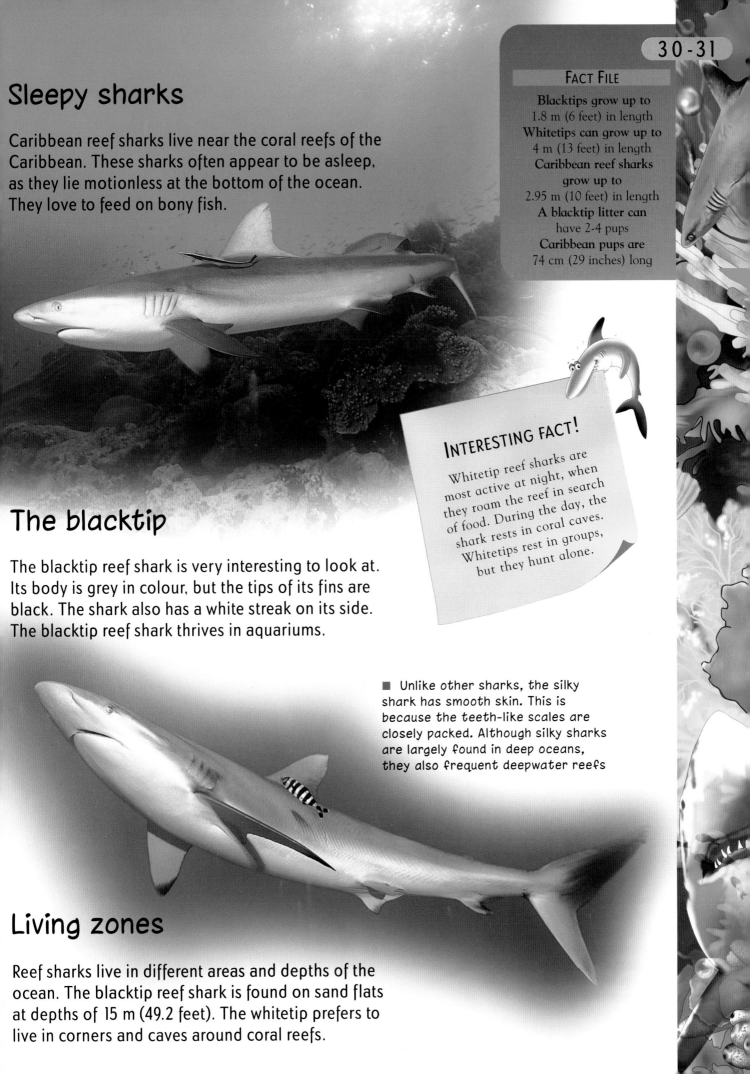

# Sleepy sharks

Caribbean reef sharks live near the coral reefs of the Caribbean. These sharks often appear to be asleep, as they lie motionless at the bottom of the ocean. They love to feed on bony fish.

FACT FILE

Blacktips grow up to 1.8 m (6 feet) in length
Whitetips can grow up to 4 m (13 feet) in length
Caribbean reef sharks grow up to 2.95 m (10 feet) in length
A blacktip litter can have 2-4 pups
Caribbean pups are 74 cm (29 inches) long

# The blacktip

The blacktip reef shark is very interesting to look at. Its body is grey in colour, but the tips of its fins are black. The shark also has a white streak on its side. The blacktip reef shark thrives in aquariums.

INTERESTING FACT!

Whitetip reef sharks are most active at night, when they roam the reef in search of food. During the day, the shark rests in coral caves. Whitetips rest in groups, but they hunt alone.

■ Unlike other sharks, the silky shark has smooth skin. This is because the teeth-like scales are closely packed. Although silky sharks are largely found in deep oceans, they also frequent deepwater reefs

# Living zones

Reef sharks live in different areas and depths of the ocean. The blacktip reef shark is found on sand flats at depths of 15 m (49.2 feet). The whitetip prefers to live in corners and caves around coral reefs.

# Angelsharks

Angelsharks have flat bodies, which make them look very much like rays. They often bury themselves in sand or mud, and all one can see are their eyes and the top of their bodies.

Eye

Spiracle

Pectoral fin

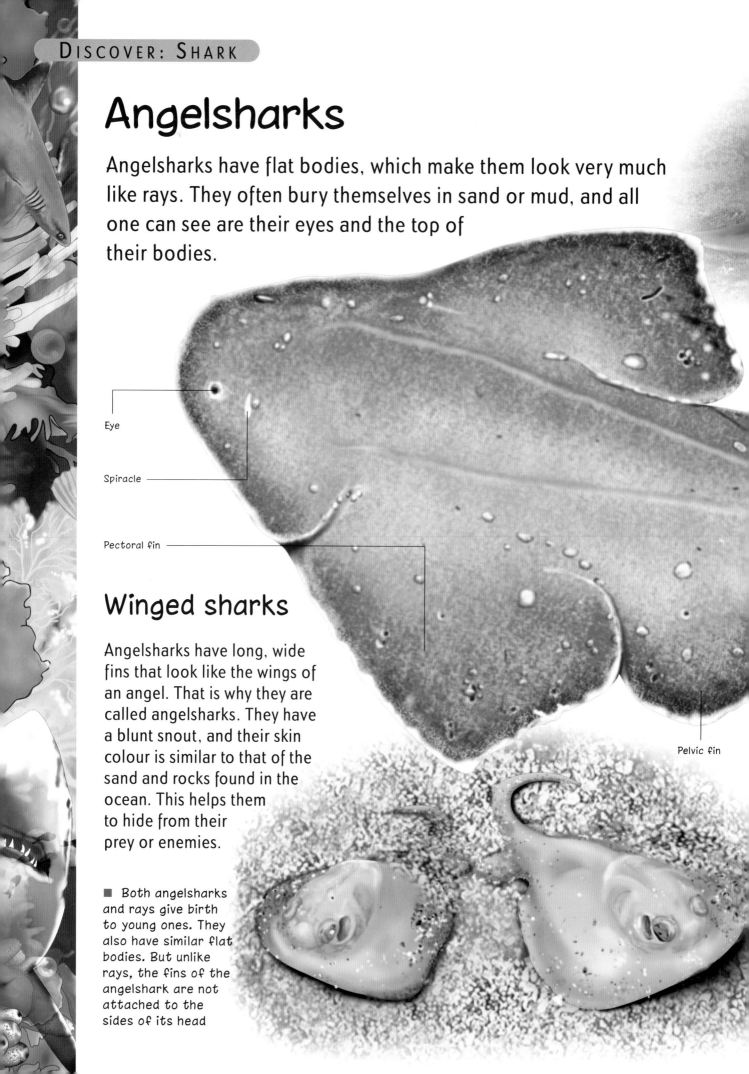

Pelvic fin

## Winged sharks

Angelsharks have long, wide fins that look like the wings of an angel. That is why they are called angelsharks. They have a blunt snout, and their skin colour is similar to that of the sand and rocks found in the ocean. This helps them to hide from their prey or enemies.

■ Both angelsharks and rays give birth to young ones. They also have similar flat bodies. But unlike rays, the fins of the angelshark are not attached to the sides of its head

## FACT FILE

Can grow up to
2 m (6.5 feet)
Number of babies
8-13 pups
Found at depths of up to
1,300 m (4,300 feet)
Can be as heavy as
27 kg (60 pounds)
Pups born at depths of
18.3-27.4 m (60-90 feet)

# Hunting by surprise

The angelshark hides in the sand and rocks,
waiting for its prey. Just as a fish swims by, the
shark pounces on it suddenly. The angelshark
eats fish, crustaceans and molluscs.
It has small and sharp teeth.

First dorsal fin

Second dorsal fin

Caudal fin

## INTERESTING FACT!

Angelsharks are not
really dangerous
if left in peace. But they
can bite if you step on
them. That's why they are
sometimes called
sand devils!

# Bottom dwellers

Angelsharks live at the
bottom of the ocean
and prefer warm waters.
They are mostly found in
the Pacific and Atlantic
Oceans. Angelsharks
are not fast swimmers,
but their prey is often
even slower!

■ The angelshark feeds on a
variety of reef fish including
croakers, groupers and flatfish

# Hammerheads

Hammerhead sharks are unique creatures, and can be easily spotted, even from a distance. They have a flat and rectangular head, which resembles a hammer. There are many types of hammerhead sharks. They can be differentiated by their "hammers"!

## Heady features

The eyes of the hammerhead shark are placed at the ends of its distinct head. The eyes can be as far apart as 1 m (3.3 feet), allowing the shark to view a larger area. Its flat head also helps the shark to keep its balance, as its side fins are very short.

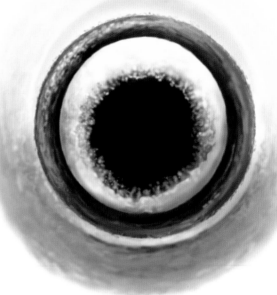

Hammerhead Eye

## Little differences

The great hammerhead has a straight head with a slight notch in the centre. The scalloped hammerhead has rounded corners on its head, while the smooth hammerhead has a broad and flat head without a notch. The bonnethead is smaller, with a shovel-shaped head.

■ The upper side of the hammerhead is dark brown, light grey or even olive in colour, while its belly is white

■ The great hammerhead migrates seasonally, moving to cooler waters during the summer

### FACT FILE

Can grow up to
6.1 m (20 feet)
Can be as heavy as
230 kg (507 pounds)
Can live up to
20-30 years
Found at depths of
300 m (984 feet)
Number of babies
6-42 pups per litter
Total attacks
Around 35 attacks per year
Fatal attacks
Rare

## INTERESTING FACT!

Angelfish act as official cleaners to hammerhead sharks. They pick up parasites from the sharks' skin and even inside their mouths. Interestingly, the hammerhead does not eat these cleaners!

## Home sweet home

Hammerheads can be found across many areas. They can live at depths of 300 m (984 feet) and can also be found in shallow coastal areas, including lagoons. They are usually found in the Mediterranean Sea and the Atlantic, Pacific and Indian Oceans.

Stingray

## Meal time

Hammerhead sharks eat crabs and fish. But their favourite food is stingray. The shark pins the stingray down using its "hammer". It feeds after sundown and hunts along the seafloor as well as near the surface. Large hammerheads also eat smaller ones.

# Sharks with a Difference

The world under the ocean is a curious place. It is home to many living creatures of all shapes, colours and sizes. Sharks, too, belong to this wonderful world. Ornate wobbegongs, carpet sharks and horn sharks are just some of the odd members of the shark family.

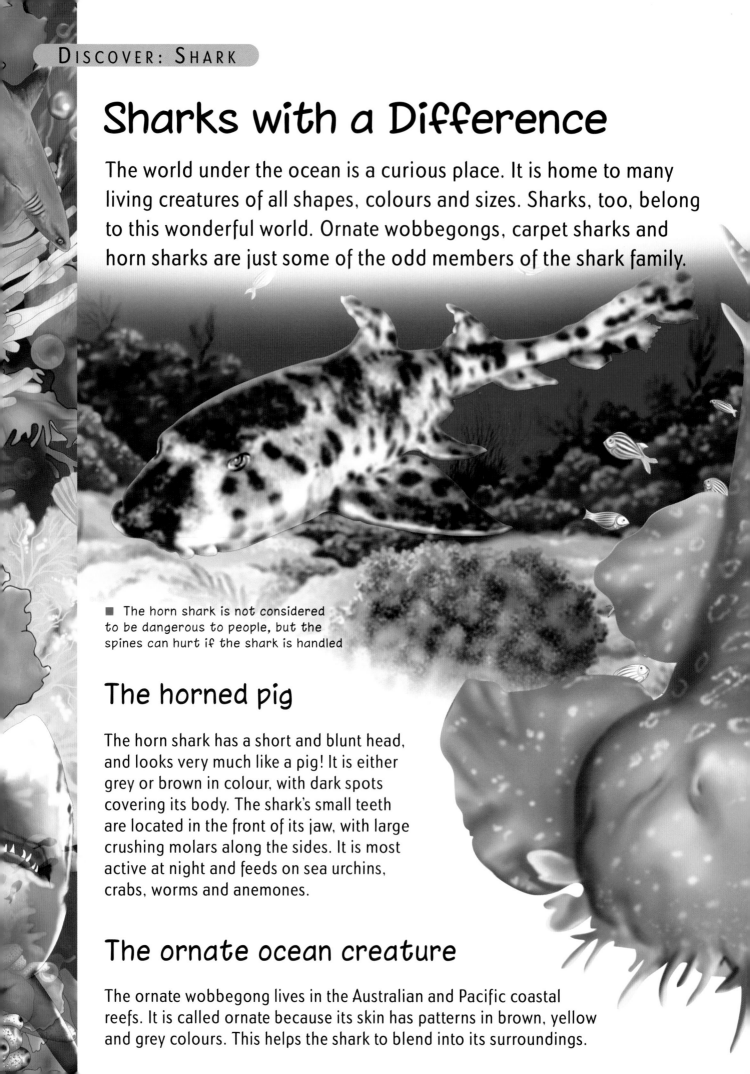

■ The horn shark is not considered to be dangerous to people, but the spines can hurt if the shark is handled

## The horned pig

The horn shark has a short and blunt head, and looks very much like a pig! It is either grey or brown in colour, with dark spots covering its body. The shark's small teeth are located in the front of its jaw, with large crushing molars along the sides. It is most active at night and feeds on sea urchins, crabs, worms and anemones.

## The ornate ocean creature

The ornate wobbegong lives in the Australian and Pacific coastal reefs. It is called ornate because its skin has patterns in brown, yellow and grey colours. This helps the shark to blend into its surroundings.

# Baiting for food

The wobbegong has worm-like projections around its mouth. The shark uses these to suck its prey into the mouth. Like the angelshark, the wobbegong also surprises its victims by camouflaging itself at the bottom of the ocean.

■ This varied carpet shark is a relative of the whale shark. But there are very few similarities between the two. The varied carpet shark is small and has a distinctive black `collar` with white spots

The ornate wobbegong

## INTERESTING FACT!

The horn shark's egg cases are curiously shaped, with a spiral like a screw. Each case contains one pup and takes from six to nine months to hatch.

# Goblins in water

The goblin shark has an unusual snout, which is long, flat and pointed. The jaws point out when the shark eats, making it look very peculiar indeed! It has soft, pale and pinkish-grey skin.

■ Little is known about goblin sharks, but it is believed that they are slow swimmers

# All in the Family

Sharks have many relatives in the ocean. One of their closest cousins is the ray. Sharks and rays actually had the same ancestors about 200 million years ago.

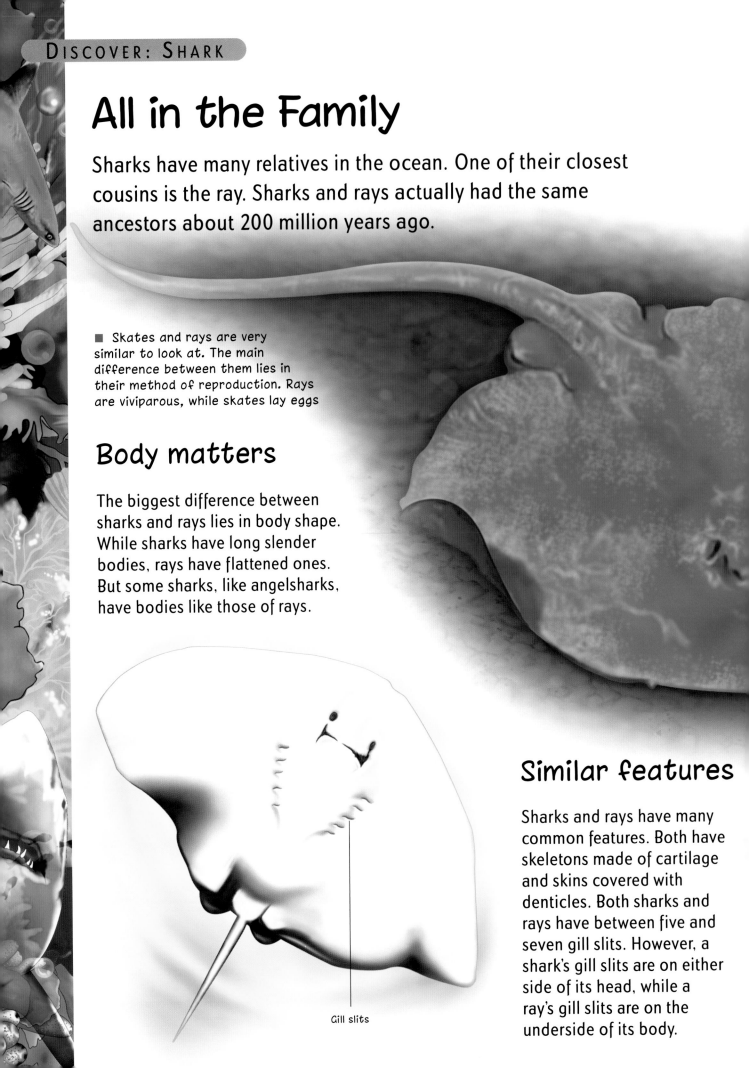

■ Skates and rays are very similar to look at. The main difference between them lies in their method of reproduction. Rays are viviparous, while skates lay eggs

## Body matters

The biggest difference between sharks and rays lies in body shape. While sharks have long slender bodies, rays have flattened ones. But some sharks, like angelsharks, have bodies like those of rays.

Gill slits

## Similar features

Sharks and rays have many common features. Both have skeletons made of cartilage and skins covered with denticles. Both sharks and rays have between five and seven gill slits. However, a shark's gill slits are on either side of its head, while a ray's gill slits are on the underside of its body.

**FACT FILE**

**Types of rays**
over 350
**The biggest ray is the**
Manta ray: its wings
measure over
6.1 m (20 feet)
**Manta rays weigh**
**more than**
1,360 kg (3,000 pounds)
**The smallest ray is the**
Shortnose electric ray
It has a wingspan of only
10 cm (4 inches)
**The shortnose electric**
**ray weighs only**
0.5 kg (1 pound)

■ Manta rays are scary to look at and are often called devil rays. But in reality, manta rays are playful and splash around in the water!

## Swimming skills

Sea creatures have unique styles of swimming. For instance, rays flap their big side fins in order to swim. But sharks use their much smaller fins for just lifting and steering. They use their tails to move around in water.

■ Like the sawshark pup, the saw of a young sawfish is covered in a protective membrane to avoid hurting the mother when she gives birth

## Name game

Like most big families, sharks and their relatives have similar names, as do sawfish and sawsharks. But often, there is very little similarity between the two. For example, the sawshark is brown, while the sawfish is light blue in colour. Moreover, the sawfish does not have barbels in the middle of its "saw".

**INTERESTING FACT!**

Many rays have spines on their tails, which can sting other animals. These spines can be poisonous too. Some rays have long and whip-like tails, while others have shorter ones.

# Shark Attack!

Over the years, shark attacks have caught the imagination of filmmakers and fiction writers. The image of a shark with its huge mouth wide open, flashing its deadly teeth, has thrilled many a movie goer. But not all sharks are a threat to us. In fact, most sharks don't even like the taste of humans!

## Not always deadly

Usually, shark attacks do not result in death or serious injury. Sharks only attack humans out of fear. Some attacks are also by accident, when a shark mistakes human surfers for seals!

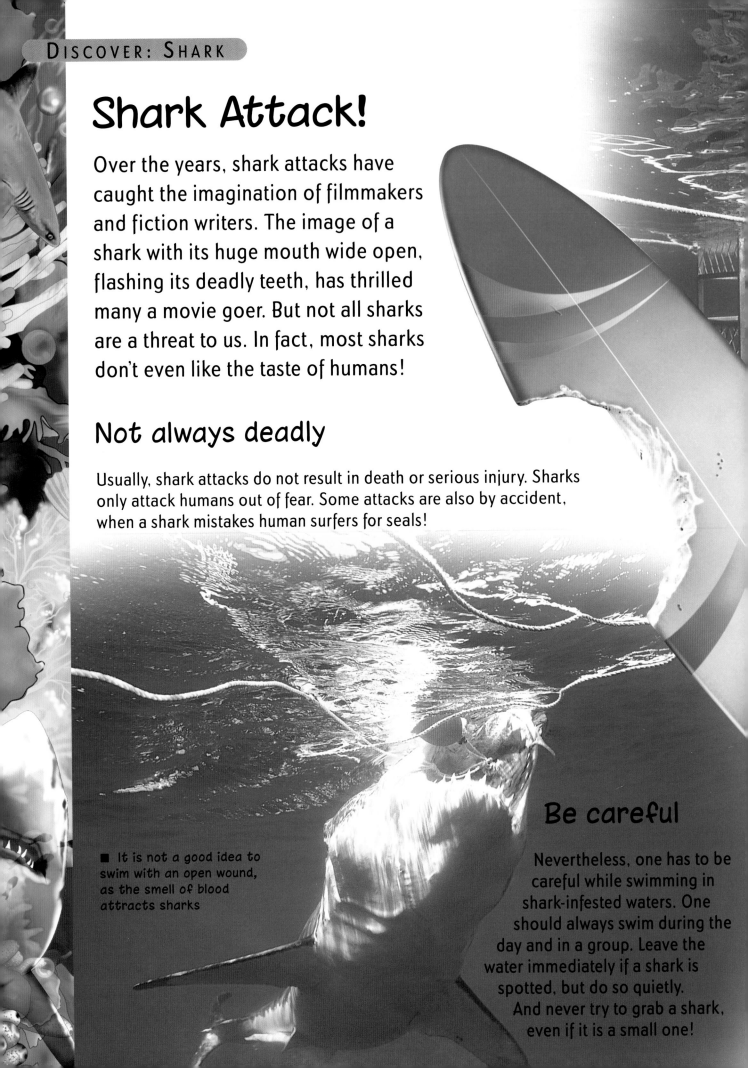

■ It is not a good idea to swim with an open wound, as the smell of blood attracts sharks

## Be careful

Nevertheless, one has to be careful while swimming in shark-infested waters. One should always swim during the day and in a group. Leave the water immediately if a shark is spotted, but do so quietly. And never try to grab a shark, even if it is a small one!

**ANNUAL DATA**
Total shark attacks
75-100
Unprovoked attacks
Around 50
Provoked attacks
15-20
Fatal attacks
11-15
Most number of attacks
recorded in:
US (over 30 attacks
every year)

■ Sharks are curious animals. They will survey a man in a cage, even though they cannot attack him!

## INTERESTING FACT!

People are more likely to die from bee stings or dog bites than to be killed by sharks! In fact, more than 90 per cent of those attacked by sharks manage to survive.

## Warning bells

If you upset a shark by trespassing in its territory, it usually warns you before attacking. It shakes its head and swims with its back hunched and snout pointing up. This is called agonistic display. If such movements are seen, one should swim away before it's too late.

## Most dangerous

There are four sharks that are particularly dangerous to humans. These are the great white, tiger, bull and oceanic whitetip sharks. Seventeen other types of sharks have also attacked humans, but they are dangerous only if threatened or disturbed. These include lemon, hammerhead, blacktip reef, nurse, wobbegong, sandtiger and spitting sharks.

■ California has one of the highest attack rates by the great white in the world, but deaths are very rare. Most of the attacks are on surfers and divers

# Endangered Sharks

Sharks are the kings of the oceans, for no other animal eats them. They are scary creatures, for they can attack, and sometimes even kill, humans. But today, sharks have much to fear from humans. Different parts of sharks, like the skin, fins and flesh, are used for various purposes.

## In danger

Due to the wide-scale killing of sharks, there has been a drop in the shark population. In fact, many have become endangered. They are so few in number that if we don't stop hunting them down, none will be left. To protect such sharks, many countries have made it illegal to kill sharks.

## Just a bycatch

Some sharks are caught by accident, as ships and fishermen try to catch other fish. A shark caught in this manner is called a bycatch. People are now working on ways to stop these accidental killings.

### INTERESTING FACT!

You can adopt a shark! Adopted sharks are specially tagged, so that you can track their movements. Shark adoption is a great way to support and protect sharks.

■ Sharks usually attack us only if we disturb them, but humans follow and hunt sharks even as a sport

# Many a product

Sharks are used in a variety of man-made products. Shark scales are removed from the skin and the hide is used to make luxurious leather. The liver oil of some sharks contains large amounts of Vitamin A. Until the late 1940s, such sharks were hunted in large numbers for Vitamin A.

■ Shark-liver oil contains more Vitamin A than cod-liver oil

■ Shark-liver oil is even used in the manufacture of lipsticks and other cosmetics

# Soupy tales

Some people also eat the flesh of sharks. In Great Britain, dogfish sharks are often used in the preparation of fish and chips. The Chinese use dried shark fins to make a popular and expensive soup.

■ Fins used in soups are obtained in a cruel manner. Fishermen drag off living sharks from the sea and slice off their fins and tails. The wounded sharks are then thrown back into the water, where they bleed to death

# Glossary

**Agonistic:** Eager to fight; agitated; aggressive.

**Anatomy:** The structure of the body of an animal or plant, or any of its parts.

**Barbel:** Thin, whisker-like organs found near the mouth of certain fish and sharks.

**Bask:** To lie in warmth or soak up the sun.

**Biologist:** A scientist or an expert who studies living organisms.

**Cartilage:** A tough, elastic tissue found in the ears and nose.

**Coastline:** The boundary of a sea shore, or coast.

**Contract:** To reduce in size; shrink.

**Crustaceans:** Any of the creatures, such as crabs, lobsters and shrimps, which belong to the class Crustacea.

**Evolution:** The gradual change in an organism to adapt itself to its environment.

**Expand:** To increase in size.

**Gills:** The organ that fish use to breathe.

**Illegal:** Against the law.

**Jaws:** The bones inside the mouth in which teeth are fixed.

**Lagoon:** A shallow lake which is cut off from the sea by coral reefs or sand bars.

**Liver:** A reddish-brown organ in animals that plays an important role in digestion.

**Membrane:** A thin fibrous tissue that covers or lines cells and organs in animals and plants.

**Molar:** A tooth that grinds food.

**Mollusc:** Invertebrates, such as snails, slugs, octopuses, squids, clams and mussels.

**Nictitating membrane:** A thin fold of skin under the eyelids that can be used to cover the eyes. It is usually found in reptiles, birds and certain mammals.

**Notch:** A V-shaped cut.

**Plankton:** Tiny plants and animals that are found floating on the surface of seas and lakes.

**Predatory:** The tendency or characteristic of an animal to hunt other animals for food.

**Radiate:** To send out, or emit.

**Remora:** A long, flat fish with spiny fins found in the ocean. It attaches itself to other fish and rocks underwater with the help of sucking discs on the top of its head.

**Requiem shark:** Any shark belonging to the Carcharhinidae family. This includes the tiger shark and the lemon shark.

**Scavenger:** An animal or bird that feeds on already dead or decaying matter.

**Temperate:** Moderate or mild in temperature. Not too cold or too hot.

**Tendrils:** Long thread-like structures.

**Torpedo:** A cigar-shaped underwater missile that is usually launched from a submarine, aircraft or ship.

# Index